WORLD WAR II

The Full Story

Life in the War

Published by Brown Bear Books Ltd
4877 N. Circulo Bujia
Tucson, AZ 85718
USA

and

First Floor
9-17 St. Albans Place
London N1 0NX

ISBN: 978-1-78121-233-2

Library of Congress Cataloging-in-Publication
Data available upon request

Managing Editor: Tim Cooke
Designer: Lynne Lennon
Picture Manager: Sophie Mortimer
Editorial Director: Lindsey Lowe
Design Manager: Keith Davis
Children's Publisher: Anne O'Daly
Production Director: Alastair Gourlay

Manufactured in the United States of America

CPSIA compliance information: Batch# AG/5566

Picture Credits

All images The Robert Hunt Library, except; 29,
30, 37b, Corbis/Bettman; 21, Getty Images/Fred
Stein Archive; 18, 20, Getty Images/The LIFE Images
Collection; 42, 43, Getty Images/Popperfoto;
23, Getty Images/Three Lions; 5tr, Imperial War
Museum; 25, iStockphoto; 8, 11, 12/13, 28, U.S.
Library of Congress; 31, U.S. National Archives.

Brown Bear Books Ltd. has made every effort to contact the
copyright holder. If you have any information please email
licensing@brownbearbooks.co.uk

All other photographs and artworks © Brown Bear Books Ltd.

CONTENTS

INTRODUCTION

World War II touched the lives of millions of people all around the globe. For the millions of men—and many women—who served in the military, life could occasionally be dangerous and stressful. Most of the time, however, it was simply boring. Many people were conscripted into the armed forces against their will. The governments of the United States and Britain made great efforts to maintain the morale of military personnel and civilians so that they would remain confident of ultimate victory. They tried to make soldiers' lives as comfortable as possible by ensuring that medical care for the wounded was as good as possible, providing entertainment, and ensuring that men at the front were kept in contact with people at home whenever possible.

Civilian Life

On the home front, people's lives were also shaped by the conflict. In Europe, hundreds of thousands of civilians were displaced from their homes by fighting or

➜ An industrial city in Germany comes under attack during a U.S. bombing raid.

➔ A young boy holds a toy for comfort after a bomb raid on London has destroyed his home.

came under enemy bombardment. Even where there was no fighting, families found their normal daily routines changed beyond recognition. With so many men away fighting, women had to take on a wider range of roles and children often had to look after themselves. The war touched every aspect of daily life, from the classroom to the workplace.

World of Propaganda

On all sides, people received information about the war from their governments. Movies, posters, and radio shows all encouraged patriotic ideas. Governments were careful to forbid any expression of dissent, or suggestions that the war might end in anything other than victory.

PROPAGANDA AND MORALE

Propaganda is information intended to shape people's ideas. During wartime, governments used any means they could to keep their citizens confident of victory.

Governments set out to influence how people viewed the war by controlling how they received information about the conflict. Reports in newspapers were carefully censored, for example, so that they did not undermine people's belief in ultimate victory. Poster campaigns and patriotic movies also helped to encourage people to have a positive view of the future. Propaganda took many forms. It included patriotic symbols such as flags, military parades, and the types of song played on radio stations. In both Allied and Axis countries, governments set up new departments to control the flow of news and information. World War II witnessed some of the biggest propaganda campaigns in history.

➡ Nazi troops with swastikas make a show of force at a party rally.

➜ Adolf Hitler was often depicted wearing militaristic clothes, even though he was a civilian.

Nazi Propaganda

In Germany, the Nazi Party perfected the use of propaganda. Adolf Hitler believed that propaganda could persuade people to believe anything. In his book, *Mein Kampf* (1924), Hitler claimed that Allied propaganda at the end of World War I (1914–1918) had persuaded the

Ein Volk, ein Reich, ein Führer!

NAZI RALLIES

Some of the most powerful and theatrical propaganda events were organized by the Nazi Joseph Goebbels. The architect Albert Speer created a dramatic arena in Nuremberg where the yearly Nazi Party congress was staged. Thousands of Nazis marched in unison, while huge crowds listened to speeches given by the party leaders.

Germans to stop supporting the army, which then surrendered. In fact, the army had surrendered because defeat had become inevitable. Nevertheless, the view that the army could have fought on was popular in Germany in the 1920s.

Hitler thought that propaganda did not have to be true to be effective. He also believed that people were more likely to believe bigger lies than small ones. If a lie was big enough, no one would think it had been made up.

Propaganda Chief

When the Nazis came to power in 1933, the man responsible for putting Hitler's beliefs into practice was Joseph Goebbels.

↑ This American poster uses Hitler's own arguments to try and persuade U.S. citizens to support the war.

CHARLES DE GAULLE

The French army officer Charles de Gaulle escaped to London after the Germans invaded France in 1940. He founded the Free French to oppose the Vichy regime's collaboration with Germany. De Gaulle was a figurehead for Allied propaganda. The Free French grew to include some 300,000 fighters, including members of the French Resistance.

He had been in charge of Nazi propaganda since 1929. Goebbels developed recognizable Nazi symbols, such as the swastika, which was originally a religious symbol in Hinduism and Buddhism, the eagle, and the laurel leaf wreath. He put on huge Nazi Party rallies with thousands of uniformed Nazis carrying banners. Goebbels was also responsible for creating a poster that featured Hitler with the slogan, "One people, one empire, one leader." The image became so popular that Germans hung it on the walls of their homes, offices, and schools.

One of the Nazis' biggest propaganda events was the Olympic Games, which were held in Berlin in 1936. The Germans saw the games as an opportunity to show the world how efficient German society was and also to prove the racial superiority of the Germanic peoples. When the African-American athlete Jesse Owens beat the home favorite Lutz Lang in the long jump, Hitler refused to present Owens with the Olympic gold medal.

Ministry of Propaganda

Goebbels' Propaganda Ministry had two main purposes: to persuade Germans of the need to expand their territory into an empire that stretched across central and eastern Europe; and to convince Germans that they were the *Herrenvolk*, or master race. The Nazis blamed Germany's economic problems on the Jews, who were portrayed as being subhuman. Germany's rapid victories across Europe in the early years of the war helped reinforce the idea that the Germans were indeed superior to their enemies. Goebbels produced a poster that declared "No one can get past the German soldier."

After Hitler invaded the Soviet Union in June 1941, Nazi propaganda switched to attacking the Soviets' communist beliefs and the threat they posed to the German way of life. After a whole German army had surrendered at Stalingrad in the southwestern Soviet Union in January

⬇ A British soldier and a French civilian work together in this propaganda poster for the Free French.

1943, German propaganda became less effective. As Germany's enemies closed in on both sides in 1945, propaganda became useless. German civilians could see for themselves that their soldiers were close to defeat.

Allied Propaganda

Allied propaganda was far less sophisticated than that of the Nazis. It was also more difficult to control information in democracies than was the case in totalitarian states. The British set up two propaganda departments. One produced propaganda aimed at demoralizing Germany and the territories it had occupied. The other, the Ministry of Information, set out to encourage the British public.

Propaganda inside Britain tried to prepare people for the possibility of the Germans launching a gas attack at any time. This meant people carrying a gas mask at all times. There were regular air-raid drills. In fact, no gas attack ever happened. Instead, from September 1940 the Germans began to bomb British cities at night in an intensive nine-month campaign known as the Blitz.

The Ministry of Information produced posters that were meant to be an effective way to give people information. There were "list" posters giving details such as where people could get meals if their homes had been bombed or how to get travel vouchers. Other posters warned against the dangers of gossip and another reminded people about the need to keep life as normal as possible. It read "Keep Calm and Carry On."

➤ This Canadian poster shows a Canadian beaver with a British lion with a cigar, like Winston Churchill's.

← President Roosevelt is helped from a car. Images like this were rarely seen.

for "V," or "victory." During the war, many people came to trust the BBC as being the most reliable and accurate source of information about the current state of the war.

American Propaganda

For most Americans, the fighting seemed very distant. To keep Americans engaged with the war effort, U.S. propaganda concentrated on reminding Americans of why the war was so important and how the outcome might affect them.

A Media Campaign

Radio played a key role in the propaganda war. The secret Political Warfare Executive was set up in August 1941 to undermine the Axis powers. It set up radio stations to broadcast messages to enemy soldiers and dropped leaflets in occupied territories about the Allied progress. The aim was to undermine German morale, but there is no real proof that this tactic worked.

The British Broadcasting Corporation or BBC (known then as the Home Service) sent coded messages to agents in France and other countries. It started its messages by playing the first four notes of Beethoven's Symphony No. 5. Its rhythm was the Morse code signal

FRANKLIN D. ROOSEVELT

Images of President Roosevelt were controlled to hide the fact that polio had left him unable to walk without sticks or leg braces. The government thought it was important in wartime to portray him as being physically strong. His disability was never a secret, but the press helped to ensure it was never too obvious.

KEY PEOPLE

➤ Propaganda put forward many different messages. Some, like this poster, urged Americans to stay out of the war.

Propaganda also had to convince many Americans that it was worth being involved in the war at all. After the end of World War I in 1918, most Americans believed that the loss of almost 120,000 dead had been too high a price to pay for what was essentially a European war. Americans were reluctant to enter another war, and embarked on a period of "isolationism" in the 1920s. The country tried to keep out of international affairs. By the time war started in Europe in 1939, the United States had also been in an economic depression for a decade. Many Americans did not want to become involved in the war, despite the support President Franklin D. Roosevelt offered

KEY THEMES

OFFICE OF WAR INFORMATION

The Office of War Information (OWI) was created in June 1942. It set out to explain the dangers of fascism to American civilians. At the same time, it promoted the image of President Franklin D. Roosevelt—both at home and overseas—as being the leader of the free world.

The OWI used any means it could to spread its positive messages: posters, movies, radio broadcasts, even postage stamps. One popular symbol it employed was a famous "V" for "victory," which was shaped by the wings of a stylized American eagle on posters and stamps.

the Allies. It was only when the Japanese unexpectedly bombed Pearl Harbor on December 7, 1941, that Americans wanted to join the war.

New Situation

The anger and outrage Americans felt at the Pearl Harbor bombing was fueled by government propaganda. Its aim was to boost national morale and confidence, even though America had entered the war on the back foot after being attacked. The government set up

> " It was a terrifying, terrifying thing. Just the sound of the troops arriving on specially metalled (asphalted) roads, goosestepping with specially metalled shoes. I was frightened by the power of it, the power that madman had over the crowd. "
>
> Daphne Brock
> British schoolgirl
> watching Hitler at a
> Nazi rally, 1930s

the Office of War Information (OWI) in 1942. Its job was to educate Americans about the dangers of fascism. The OWI created posters that were put up in public places such as schools, restaurants and railroad stations. The posters were distributed and displayed by members of volunteer defense councils. Well-known artists, such as Norman Rockwell, created positive images for the posters; some images even appeared on postage stamps. Another U.S. government organization, the Bureau of Motion

ВПЕРЕД! НА ЗАПАД!

← This Soviet poster from 1942 has the slogan "Forward to the West!"

Pictures, was established in Hollywood to ensure that movies reinforced a positive image of American involvement in the war. In the three years of the Bureau's existence, it altered more than 500 films to give a greater boost to civilian morale.

Newspapers did their part, too, by agreeing not to show photographs of dead soldiers. Radio stations also broadcast uplifting music to service personnel in Europe and the Pacific.

Soviet Propaganda

Propaganda played a different role in the Soviet Union. Since 1923, Joseph Stalin had controlled the Soviet Union with an iron hand. He used propaganda to portray a very different reality from the suffering experienced by the Soviet people on a daily basis.

Many Soviet citizens could not read and few had radios, so the Soviet propaganda campaign was carried on mainly through the use of simple, graphic posters. Soviet artists developed a distinctive, modern style, using flat colors and hard edges. Most posters featured both an image and lettering. The lettering was large and usually

spelled out a slogan, but in most cases it was not vital to understanding the meaning of the image.

Stalin knew that most Russians did not have any great loyalty to his Communist Party. For this reason, many of the posters instead appealed to their loyalty to the Russian nation. Posters portrayed heroes who had helped defend the nation in the

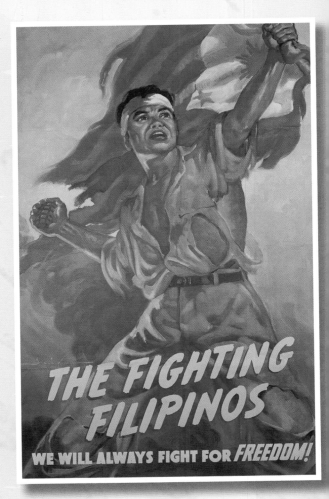

→ The United States produced this poster to inspire Filipino resistance to the Japanese.

THE FIGHTING FILIPINOS

WE WILL ALWAYS FIGHT FOR *FREEDOM!*

BOERI · INDIANI · EGIZIANI · ARABI · IRLANDESI

Per la Gran Bretagna tutte le razze e tutti i popoli sono uguali

← This Italian poster shows the British hanging anyone who wanted freedom from British rule.

Tokyo Rose

For U.S. servicemen in the Pacific, the most familiar form of Japanese propaganda came in regular broadcasts by "Tokyo Rose." The Japanese used English-speaking women to broadcast radio propaganda from Tokyo, telling Allied soldiers across the Pacific region that defeat was coming. There were a number of "Roses." The most famous was Iva Toguri, an American detained in Japan and forced to broadcast.

past, such as the medieval prince Alexander Nevsky. The posters appealed to the Russians' love of what they called "Mother Russia."

Japanese Propaganda

Japanese propaganda concentrated on portraying the Japanese as a "pure" people and its enemies as impure. It used posters to show how powerful Japan was. It also tried to convince other peoples across Asia that Japan could liberate them from European colonial rule. This view was more popular in Japan than elsewhere in Asia.

MOTHER RUSSIA

The image of Mother Russia was powerful in Russian history and folklore. She was portrayed as a *babushka*, a kind of nurse with whom most Russians were familiar from their childhoods. In the same way a babushka looked after children, Mother Russia was responsible for protecting the land. After victory in the war, statues of Mother Russia were set up to celebrate.

KEY PEOPLE

CIVILIAN LIFE

Around the world, the impact of the war changed daily lives. Families were separated, people faced shortages, homes were bombed, and entertainment was limited.

For civilians, life changed in many ways, depending on where they lived. Some people found themselves under foreign occupation. Others lost their homes to bombing and became refugees. They became known as "displaced persons," or DPs. People fleeing the fighting in regions such as northeastern France, Belgium, or Poland wandered randomly through Europe, seeking a safe place to live.

In Britain, so many people were bombed out of their homes during the Blitz of September 1940 to May 1941 that local authorities could not cope. The victims could go to centers to receive food, drink, and clothing, but usually had to find their own accommodation. Many moved in with relatives or friends.

→ Children in London sit in the ruins of their home after a German bombing raid.

← Children arrive at a rural railroad station in England after leaving a city.

EVACUATION

The British evacuated millions of children from cities that were in danger of being bombed. When children arrived in the countryside, they were allocated to new homes. Often, they were separated from their brothers or sisters. Some children were lucky enough to stay with kind families; others were used like servants. Many parents missed their children and brought them back to the city.

In Germany and Japan, too, families were caught up later in the war in massive Allied bombing raids on cities such as Dresden and Tokyo. Some refugees, particularly European Jews who had managed to escape Nazi controlled areas, left Europe for North or South America.

Family Life

Even those civilians not directly affected by the conflict were affected in other ways. They suffered from food and

→ A young boy leads his class in the Pledge of Allegiance in Slocum, Oregon.

clothing shortages and experienced rationing, as governments prioritized industry to support the war effort. Families everywhere were affected by the fact that most able-bodied men were drafted into the services, leaving women to look after the children and often also to earn money to support their families. Many women joined the workforce for the first time. They took factory jobs making armaments or military hardware, but they also did other jobs, such as teaching, driving trucks, and working in the fields.

Children in Wartime

One of the other groups in civilian society to be affected by the war was children. In Germany, young boys

KEY THEMES

SHORTAGES AND RATIONING

Essential goods, such as metals and gasoline, were needed for war industries, so they were rationed for civilians. There were also less obvious shortages. Paper was in short supply, so people gave up sending greetings cards. People gave up their dogs to the military canine corps, and there were no binoculars to spare for birdwatchers. Even tennis balls were in short supply because industry needed rubber.

← Jewish refugees wait on the quayside to board a ship bound for North America.

were women. The same was true in the United States and most other Allied countries. When school buildings were damaged, classes were held in pubs or in church halls. Lessons were changed to include drills for what to do in an air raid or activities such as knitting clothes for troops. Teachers and students often also studied the progress of the war together.

Students often found it difficult to concentrate at school if they had been kept awake by air raids the previous

who were members of the Hitler Youth served in the armed forces, particularly during the Battle of Berlin just before the end of the war. In other countries, such as Ukraine, France, and Italy, children did not fight but normal life was put on hold. Schools were damaged or destroyed, and children were more concerned about finding food for their families than about education or playing with their friends.

Keep Calm and Carry On

In Britain, meanwhile, children still had to go to school and take exams. Because many male teachers had gone to fight, most teachers that remained at home

EYEWITNESS ACCOUNT

"During this time, many families would take their children out of school at a young age—twelve years for many—so that they could go to work and help the family survive. The most popular places to work were bakeries and any place that made food. This way at least you could bring some leftover food home to your family."

Evelyn Whitaker on her mother's childhood in wartime Germany

MOVEMENTS OF PEOPLE

When the war began, many African Americans moved north to find work. Other Americans were also on the move. Many people moved to the West Coast, where there were war industries and military camps. Military bases also attracted people to the South. Travel was difficult, however, as public transportation gave priority to moving military personnel around.

Life in the United States

In the United States, war production finally brought an end to the effects of the Great Depression that had started in 1929. When war began in Europe in 1939, 15 percent of Americans were unemployed (today a normal rate of unemployment is 5 percent). By 1943, two years after the United States entered the war, unemployment stood at just 1 percent, the lowest level ever recorded.

Many of the new workers were women working in the war industries. Two million black Americans also worked in the

night. Children suffered from shortages of foods, especially treats such as candy. There was a shortage of paper, so there were few comics or children's magazines. In the evenings, few people went out because of the blackout, which was intended to obstruct German bombers by hiding light from buildings or cars. Families listened to the radio together, read books—only unillustrated books were printed—and played cards or board games. Going on vacation became rare.

→ University of California, Berkeley, students cheer at a college football game.

→ A family in New York City reads news of the surrender of Italy in September 1943.

defense industries, having moved north to find work. However, many faced discrimination and received unfair pay.

Women who had to go out to work left their children in the care of grandparents, other family members, and neighbors. Older siblings often took responsibility for looking after their younger brothers and sisters. Children also joined groups such as the Boy Scouts, which helped organize support for the war effort, such as campaigns to collect scrap metal.

Sports in Wartime

In the United States, professional sports continued as a way to keep up people's morale. Many major league baseball players were drafted, so their clubs had to recruit minor league players or rehire retired players. Many minor league teams folded. In 1943 the All-American Girl's Professional Baseball League was founded. Their games were not as popular as men's games, but more than 900,000 people watched women's league games in the last years of the war. American football teams also recruited players from the lower leagues, although there were still so few players that some teams were forced to merge.

Reporting the War

Civilians received most of their news about the fighting from newspapers. Many famous writers became war correspondents. Most correspondents worked with permission from the armed forces, and they relied on the military for transportation and protection. In return, military officials censored reports to prevent negative impressions of the action. For many reporters, censorship was unnecessary. They did not see their job as presenting a balanced view. They wanted to support the war effort, so they were happy to report a largely positive view of their own side.

The War and the Movies

Movies also took a patriotic approach to the war. At the time, the cinema was a very important means of communication. Berlin alone had more than 400 cinemas

in 1942. They showed newsreels and movies that portrayed the Western Allies and the Soviets as villains. In Britain and the United States, meanwhile, patriotic movies showed the Allies as heroic and their enemies as cruel and inhuman.

Movies were popular with civilians and soldiers alike. Even though they were often propaganda, they were enjoyable to watch. The actor John Wayne had a reputation for playing tough, honest cowboys in Western movies. Wayne starred in action movies about the war itself, such as *The Fighting Seabees* (1944) or *The Flying Tigers* (1942). He portrayed U.S. soldiers as being brave in

⬇ Female war correspondents pose during the Allied advance in northern Europe.

← Moviegoers stand in line to watch *A Yank on the Burma Road*, a movie from 1942.

A few movies rose above the level of propaganda to become classics. They included *Casablanca* (1942), set in German-occupied Morocco. Humphrey Bogart and Ingrid Bergman starred as individuals facing tough moral choices. Bergman also starred with Gary Cooper in *For Whom the Bell Tolls* (1943). The movie was based on Ernest Hemingway's novel about the Spanish Civil War (1936–1939). It examined freedom and democracy, the causes for which the Allies were also fighting in World War II.

the face of huge odds. The soldiers Wayne played were long-suffering, loyal, and self-sufficient. Wayne's war heroes had many of the same qualities as the cowboys of earlier Western movies.

From Propaganda to Classics

Some movies were more obviously escapist. They usually did not make any reference to what was going on in the war. Such movies included famous Walt Disney feature-length cartoons, such as *Fantasia* and *Pinocchio* (both 1940), and *Bambi* (1942). *Mrs. Miniver* (1942), a Hollywood movie about an English family facing the hardships of wartime, was criticized for showing an idealized version of Britain, partly in order to encourage American support for the alliance with the British.

LOVE OF BOOKS

One of the most popular pastimes for civilians and soldiers was reading. The bestsellers included *A Tree Grows in Brooklyn* (1943) by Betty Smith, an inspirational novel about an Irish American family in Brooklyn in the 1920s and 1930s. Novels were printed in tiny print on thin paper because paper was scarce. Special lightweight editions of books were printed and sent free to military personnel overseas.

SOLDIER LIFE

For the millions of military personnel, everyday life had many similarities no matter what side they were on. Home comforts and individual choice were rare.

UNSERE
Luftwaffe

World War II needed millions of people to fight on both sides. No army had enough soldiers to fight throughout the war and so conscription (being forced to join the military by law) was used alongside volunteers to increase numbers.

Joining the Military

Some 16 million people served in the U.S. military during the war. From Britain and its vast empire 8.7 million served, and in Germany the number in the military by the end of the war was almost 11 million. Of those, most were conscripted. They had to be trained to serve in a modern army.

Military leaders tried to employ people with civilian skills so that they did not have to be trained from scratch.

← This poster called on volunteers to join the German air force, or Luftwaffe.

ON HIS MAJESTY'S SERVICE

*I removed on _____
to the following address :— _____ (date)

Nearest Railway Station :— _____

*I have changed my name to _____

Signature _____
*Complete as necessary

FOR USE OF SERVICE AUTHORITY ONLY
This man has joined H.M. Forces as a volunteer.
_____ Unit
_____ Date

Signature _____
Rank _____

OFFICIAL PAID

The Manager,
Local Office of the
Ministry of Labour
and National Service,

KEEP THIS CARD SAFELY
NATIONAL SERVICE ACTS, 1939-1941
Certificate of Registration

Occ. Classn. No. _____
Holder's Name _____ Registration No. GNC _____
Home Address _____

Date of Birth _____ /19
Holder's Signature _____

READ THIS CAREFULLY
Care should be taken not to lose this Certificate, but in the event of loss, application for a duplicate should be made to the nearest office of the Ministry of Labour and National Service.
If you change your address, etc., you must complete the appropriate space on the other side of this certificate and post it at once. A new Certificate of Registration will then be sent to you.
If you voluntarily join H.M. Forces you should hand this certificate to the appropriate Service Officer.
You should not voluntarily give up your employment because you have been registered for military service.
This certificate must be produced on request to a constable in uniform.
A person who uses or lends this certificate or allows it to be used by any other person with intent to deceive, renders himself liable to heavy penalties.
N.S.2.
6/41

← The British issued cards to make everyone register for possible conscription.

Keeping up Morale

Military leaders knew that in order to get the best out of their forces they needed to keep up morale. Keeping a positive spirit meant that soldiers would cope better with the danger, homesickness, lack of comfort, and boredom that war brought. Reinforcing the idea that they were fighting for a moral right was another means of boosting morale. Soldiers on both sides were repeatedly taught that they were militarily and morally superior to their enemy. At the start of the war, for example, decades of

Experienced drivers, doctors, nurses, mechanics, and engineers were recruited, but there were still some jobs for which men had to be trained from scratch, such as pilots. At the start of the war, many pilots went into action while they were still not fully trained.

Recruiters found that most recruits did not have the fitness needed to fight— armies walked long distances and carried heavy loads. One of the first things virtually all new soldiers did in training was to undergo an intensive course of physical training (PT) to become fit as quickly as possible.

CONSCRIPTION

It soon became apparent that the war could not be fought by volunteers alone. Most countries turned to conscription, or forcing citizens to serve in the armed forces. This raised personnel in large numbers, but it also removed workers from their jobs, disrupted families, and brought many poor quality recruits into the armed services.

KEY THEMES

Life in the War

" There was little room to err without being critiqued. Punishment was available through extra guard duty, kitchen police, looking for matchsticks and cigarette butts, marking targets on the rifle range, oral and written reprimands, and reduction in rank. "

Vernon E. Green
U.S. 10th Infantry Rgt.,
in basic training, 1939

↑ German recruits use a form of marching called the goosestep during training.

militaristic culture had given Japanese soldiers an ingrained belief that they were superior to other fighting nations.

Boredom

Between bouts of fighting, every soldier had long periods when nothing much happened. During those periods, soldiers had to be entertained and kept busy to keep their spirits up. When they were not on the front line, they also needed to have as many home comforts as was practical. That meant somewhere dry to

→ Soldiers were encouraged by **propaganda** stories of individual heroism.

sleep, enough to eat and drink, showers, and clean clothes. Each army camp had a quartermaster whose job it was to organize the camp's living conditions.

One of the most important things for any soldier was keeping in touch with home. Every army placed huge importance on military mail. The German Army kept delivering its post right up to its surrender in 1945. U.S. servicemen received so much mail that a new method was devised to reduce the amount of paper being sent. Letters were photographed and shrunk to a tiny miniature and then sent as V-mail. When the V-mail arrived at its destination it was magnified again so the soldier could read his letter.

MEN *of* VALOR
They fight for you

"When last seen he was collecting Bren and Tommy Guns and preparing a defensive position which successfully covered the withdrawal from the beach." — Excerpt from citation awarding Victoria Cross to Lt.-Col. Merritt, South Saskatchewan Regt., Dieppe, Aug. 19, 1942

PHYSICAL FITNESS

Military commanders on both sides found that many conscripts who joined the armed services were not physically fit. They were not able to march long distances or carry gear without being exhausted. The problem was caused partly by poor food, which was then corrected by a more balanced diet in the military. Armies also introduced physical training (PT) to make men fit as quickly as possible. Units performed exercise classes together, along with frequent marching drills and demanding exercises such as assault courses.

KEY THEMES

→ The message of this U.S. poster had a serious purpose: cleanliness helped prevent disease.

Entertainment

One of the most popular ways of keeping troops happy was to put on some kind of show. Soldiers enjoyed watching movies and theatrical shows. The Entertainments National Service Association (ENSA) was formed in 1939 to keep British servicemen and women entertained. Famous singers such as Gracie Fields and actors such as Lawrence Olivier entertained the troops but sometimes troops had to make do with less famous

It's an Old American Custom

KEEP CLEAN

THESE GUYS RIGGED UP THIS SHOWER 48 HOURS AFTER MAKING A BEACH-HEAD

Take a bath every day you can

KEY THEMES

THE RED CROSS

The Red Cross was formed in 1863 to provide care for soldiers during wartime. It was active in Europe in World War II, where it helped arrange postal services for prisoners of war. It also checked that prisoners were being treated according to international rules. The Red Cross also tried to reunite families who had been displaced by fighting.

entertainers. Soldiers joked that ENSA stood for Every Night Something Awful.

United Service Organizations (USO)

In early 1941, President Franklin D. Roosevelt established the USO to provide entertainment for American troops. It had 3,000 camps around the world to give soldiers a "home away from home." The USO was much more ambitious than ENSA. It was best known for its "camp shows," when movie stars or professional entertainers, such as Bob Hope and the Andrews Sisters, visited military bases to perform. The USO put on around 300,000 shows during the war. In addition, the USO organized dances and movie shows, and had canteens with free coffee and donuts. Camps had quiet rooms for writing letters and libraries with magazines and books.

Music

Both sides realized how important music was for keeping up their forces' morale. Almost all the combatant countries set up

forces radio stations, which provided soldiers with entertainment and information. Hearing a familiar voice was a great link with home and popular songs were a morale booster. German soldiers listened to "Lili Marlene," a love song about a soldier who was away from his girlfriend. It became extremely popular among Axis soldiers because it was frequently broadcast on the German forces radio station, Radio Belgrade. British soldiers particularly liked Vera Lynn's (who was known as the forces' sweetheart) "We'll meet again." U.S. soldiers often listened to Irving Berlin's popular songs "God Bless America"

↓ U.S. corpsmen give a wounded soldier a blood transfusion in the Pacific.

← U.S. veterans sail back into New York harbor at the end of the war.

(which became an unofficial national anthem) and "Oh How I Hate to Get Up in the Morning," which Berlin often performed live in front of the troops. Both songs became standards, although they were both actually written before World War II.

Medical Care

Great strides had been made in the medical care of soldiers after the end of World War I. In World War II, far more emphasis was placed on keeping soldiers healthy in both body and mind. Doctors knew that vaccinations and tablets prevented potentially fatal diseases such as malaria. Penicillin was produced in massive quantities (some 2.3 million doses by D-Day in June 1944). It was used to prevent wounds from becoming infected by the spread of bacteria.

Treating soldiers on the battlefield and evacuating them as quickly as possible also led to a reduction in the number of deaths on the front line. During the American Civil War (1861–1865), almost 50 percent of soldiers died from their wounds. Nearly a century later, that number had fallen to just 4 percent of wounded Americans who had been admitted to hospital.

LOOKING AFTER THE WOUNDED

Modern firearms and bombs meant that huge numbers of soldiers suffered serious injuries, and medical procedures improved to keep pace. Pilots, tank crew, and sailors often had severe burns. British surgeon Sir Harold Gillies led advances in the use of plastic surgery to repair serious burns. Thousands of soldiers lost limbs in explosions, and there were improvements in the use of prosthetics for amputees. The advances were led by the U.S. Army Prosthetic Research Lab. Some of its developments are still in use.

→ A U.S. staff sergeant meets his daughter who was born while he was overseas.

Mental Health

Another big change from earlier conflicts was the realization by governments that fighting and being away from home could cause psychological damage such as depression. In World War I, soldiers suffering from depression and accused of cowardice had been executed. By the start of World War II, governments were beginning to understand that stress was an unavoidable medical condition during war. Psychological problems affected 1 in 12 of all U.S. service personnel—some 400,000 troops were so badly affected they were sent home. In the 21st century it became known that many soldiers in both wars had been suffering from a nervous condition called "shell shock."

GLOBAL WAR

Almost all of the world's nations were eventually drawn into World War II. Some tried to remain neutral, but they were usually unsuccessful.

When World War II started in September 1939, many countries declared themselves to be neutral, meaning that they would not take sides. However, as the war carried on, more and more neutral countries were involved in the conflict.

These included Norway, Holland, Luxembourg, and Belgium, which were all invaded by Germany in 1940. The countries of the Balkans were also forced into the war when Italy sided with Germany and Hitler decided to invade the Balkans' ally, the Soviet Union.

⬇ The crew of a British armored car round up Bedouin Arabs in Iraq in May 1941.

← The Spanish Blue Division were volunteers who fought with German soldiers on the Eastern Front.

Some European countries were able to remain neutral throughout the war. Spain stayed out of the war although its dictator, General Francisco Franco, was sympathetic to the Axis. Franco declared Spain a "non-belligerent" state in 1940. That meant it would not do any fighting, but Franco still sent supplies to Germany and let German submarines and aircraft use Spanish ports and airbases. Some Spanish volunteers also fought alongside German soldiers on the Eastern Front. After 1943, as the Allies gained a stronger position in the war, Franco's support for the Axis declined.

Fragile Neutrality

Ireland, Sweden, and Switzerland remained neutral throughout the war. Ireland had only been independent from Britain since 1921 and there was still resentment against the British. However, Ireland secretly supported the Allied cause. When German pilots were forced to land in Ireland, for example, they were interned. Allied pilots, on the other hand, were secretly sent to Northern Ireland—part of the United Kingdom— from where they rejoined the Allied forces. Around 100,000 Irish volunteers also served in the Allied armed forces.

For Sweden, neutrality proved hard to maintain as the Germans threatened to attack. As a compromise, the Swedes allowed German troops to use Swedish railroads. Meanwhile, the Swiss escaped German aggression largely because of its strong banking system, in which Hitler and the Nazis stored much of the gold they seized during the war. Although Portugal remained technically neutral, it helped the Axis economically and the British militarily.

Turkey remained neutral for most of the war but continued to trade with its traditional ally, Germany. Turkey finally declared war on Germany in 1945 in order to gain admission to the Allied conference founding the United Nations.

Latin America and the War

When the war began, Canada—like the other colonies of the European Allies— joined the conflict. Other nations in North and South America declared their neutrality. In October 1939, the American republics signed the Declaration of Panama. They agreed to confer if the war spread to the Americas. They also created a 300-mile (480-km) neutrality zone around the American coasts, in which they would not tolerate aggressive acts.

Many Latin American countries had some sympathy with the Axis powers because they themselves were controlled by military governments or dictatorships.

Once Germany declared war on the United States in December 1941, the U.S. government pressed Latin American countries to end diplomatic relations with the Axis. The Latin American countries had little choice but to comply because they did not want to lose U.S. economic investment. By the end of the war, Latin

➜ This photo of Dublin, Ireland, shows how the Bells laundry appealed to anti-British feeling.

← Mexican-Americans drill during training. Mexico joined the Allies in 1942, but its troops did not fight.

American neutrality had largely been abandoned in favor of support for the U.S. war effort.

The Middle East

Since the end of World War I in 1918, much of West Asia had been under foreign control. Both Britain and France had set up governments in the region, which were known as mandates. The British occupied Iraq. While Iraq's neighbor, Iran, was independent, both

KEY THEMES

IRELAND

Although Ireland was officially neutral, some Irish people sympathized with the Axis powers. They resented centuries of British colonial rule. The Irish government tried to remain balanced. It banned British ships from Irish ports, for example, and allowed Axis spies to operate freely. In secret, however, it offered subtle forms of support to the British government.

Britain and the Soviet Union had business interests in the country. In August 1941, Allied forces occupied Iran after the Germans invaded the Soviet Union. The Allies feared the Germans might attack Iran's oil reserves through the Caucasus.

Asia and Africa

Most nations in Africa and Asia became involved in the war because of their links to European empires. British colonies and members of the Commonwealth—who were former colonies—also joined the struggle. Britain's most important allies included Canada, Australia, New Zealand, and India. The Indian Army was an important source of manpower for the British Army.

Within India there was opposition to being drawn into the war. The nationalist leaders Mahatma Gandhi and Jawaharlal Nehru, together with about 20,000 of their supporters, were imprisoned for protesting the war and breaking British laws. Meanwhile, many Indian Muslims supported the conflict in the hope that in return they would earn British support for a Muslim homeland after independence.

⬇ The British King's African Rifles parade after liberating Madagascar in 1942.

← The Arab Legion formed in what is now Jordan and fought on the side of the Allies in the Middle East.

regime, although French Equatorial Africa (now Chad, Cameroon, the Central African Republic, Congo, and Gabon) came under the control of the Free French led by Charles de Gaulle.

The island of Madagascar was also a French colony. In 1942 the Allies became concerned that the Axis powers might be planning to use the island as a naval base. British forces decided to take control of the island, landing on Madagascar in May 1942.

Thailand had close ties with Japan but when Japanese troops entered Thailand a day after the Pearl Harbor attacks, the Thais soon capitulated and signed a Treaty of Alliance with Japan. Under pressure from their new allies, they declared war on Britain and the United States in January 1942.

The War in Africa

In Africa, British and French colonies provided soldiers to fight the Axis. Some fought the Italians in Ethiopia and Somaliland in East Africa. Most French colonies were loyal to the puppet Vichy

WAR IN SYRIA AND LEBANON

In the Middle East, Syria and Lebanon had been under French control since the end of World War I in 1918. They passed to Vichy France in 1940. When the French began to allow German pilots to use airfields in Syria, Britain invaded. To the surprise of the British, the Vichy troops resisted strongly, but Syria was under Allied control within a month.

END OF THE WAR

When the war finally ended, one of the priorities of the Allied governments was to get military personnel home. That required a huge amount of organization.

When World War II ended in Europe—and again when Japan surrendered in the Pacific three months later—virtually everyone involved in the fighting had just one thought: getting home. The process of demobilizing huge armies was in many ways just as complicated as the process of creating them in the first place.

By the end of the war, the United States had 12 million personnel overseas; the British had 5 million. They all wanted to go home. The Axis powers had been destroyed, so there were no authorities to organize the demobilization of German and Japanese soldiers. In most cases, they were left to get themselves home. Soviet soldiers were redirected to new tasks. Many Soviet men who had been drafted at the war's start never made it home.

➜ Crowds celebrate Victory in Europe (VE) Day in New York in 1945.

← A displaced family takes a few belongings as they move from eastern to western Germany.

Allied planning for demobilization actually began two years before Germany's defeat, when an Allied victory became certain. The British had experience of large-scale demobilization following World War I in 1918, and followed the lessons they had learned. Soldiers who had served the longest were demobilized, or demobbed, first. Some soldiers were also demobbed more quickly because their skills were needed back home. For other soldiers, however,

TREATMENT OF COLLABORATORS

Many citizens of Allied countries had cooperated with or fought for the Axis powers in the war. They were termed collaborators. In France, 120,000 officials were found guilty of treason for working for the Nazis' puppet government in Vichy. About 2,000 were executed. Women who had dated German soldiers were publicly shamed by having their heads shaved.

KEY THEMES

> " I received my officers' demob document. Throughout my six years service my conduct was described as 'exemplary.' This was a word I had not met before and I took the first opportunity to check in a dictionary and was pleased to find it was complimentary. "
>
> John Rawlings
> British infantry officer,
> demobilized in 1945

had stayed in civilian jobs while they had been away fighting. Some also found it difficult to accept that women had been working more widely and had become more financially independent. As for women in the workforce, they often found their jobs removed in order to make way for returning servicemen.

Passed in June 1944, the Servicemen's Readjustment Act, or GI Bill, changed the United States. It gave returning servicemen a no-interest loan to buy a house, $20 a week for a year while they

the process could seem slow. Frustration at waiting to go home caused rioting among U.S. personnel in the Pacific.

Getting soldiers home was just the start. An even bigger problem was helping them to readjust to life on "civvy street," or in civilian life. Discharged American and British soldiers were all given a suit, collar, and tie to be worn in job interviews. For some men, it was the first suit they ever owned. Many veterans still found it difficult to find jobs, however. They sometimes resented the men who

➡ French soldiers leave the German prisoner of war camp where they had been held.

← German civilians leave a screening of an Allied movie about Nazi atrocities.

were also still required. Their government introduced National Service—a program of compulsory enrollment for young men in the armed services. It remained in place until 1960, 15 years after the end of the war. Among other tasks, British soldiers served in the Army on the Rhine, an occupation force in Germany.

Hidden Problems

Demobilization was not an entirely positive experience for many veterans of the war. After the joyful experience of

looked for work, and access to free higher education. In the decade following the war, some 2.2 million veterans had used the bill to go to university and another 5.6 million had received other forms of training. Their new skills helped support a decade of prosperity for America in the 1950s.

The Allies could not demobilize all their soldiers. Many U.S. soldiers remained in Germany to oversee the transition to peace. In Japan, General Douglas MacArthur led a U.S. occupying force that eventually numbered 350,000, which remained for seven years. British soldiers

POTSDAM CONFERENCE

In July 1945 the Allied leaders met at Potsdam, near Berlin, to plan the postwar world. Both the United States and Britain had new leaders, Harry S. Truman and Clement Attlee, respectively. Soviet leader Joseph Stalin was able to strengthen his control over eastern Europe, which was occupied by Soviet troops. That helped shape European history for four decades.

KEY EVENTS

REFUGEES

By 1945, some 30 million Europeans were refugees. Many tried to get home, but others had nowhere left to call home. Looking after refugees was the task of the United Nations Relief and Rehabilitation Administration. It set up refugee camps and food distribution points in 17 countries. Between 1945 and 1947 it handed out 25 million tons of food to refugees and the homeless.

coming home, men faced the problems of finding work and supporting their families. Many husbands and wives found it difficult to fit back into family life. The divorce rate in the United States doubled from 1941 to 4.3 divorces per 1,000 people in 1946. The causes of this rise were complex. Some soldiers had been away for so long that either their wives had found new partners or the soldiers themselves had done so. Soldiers also had to get used to dealing with children they might not have seen for three or four years, or who might have been born

⬇ Hundreds of U.S. troops crowd the decks of the liner bringing them home from Europe.

→ A British soldier who has lost an arm in the war hugs his wife as she welcomes him back home.

soon after the men had left for Europe or the Pacific. Some found it difficult to cope.

The experience of war had also changed the soldiers, who were not the same people as they had been when they set off for the war.

Meanwhile, many women had found a new independence through their war work. They were therefore less dependent on their husbands when they returned, and often less willing to simply obey their husbands' rules.

The Cost of the War

The ongoing emotional cost of the war was only a small part of its overall cost. The destruction and loss it had caused had been on an unimaginable scale. Swathes of Europe lay in ruins, millions of people had been killed, injured, or left homeless. Europe would be divided for decades between the Soviet-occupied East and the West.

World War II had been a truly global conflict. Many countries had been involved, even if only in the latter stages.

Heavily populated areas of Europe, Asia, and Africa had become war zones. Fewer than 15 nations had remained neutral throughout the whole war.

Producing accurate casualty figures for the war remains difficult. While Britain and the United States kept careful records, Germany, Japan, and the Soviet Union did not. The most common estimate puts the war's total death toll at around 56 million people.

TIMELINE OF WORLD WAR II

1939   **September:** German troops invade and overrun Poland; Britain and France declare war on Germany; the Soviet Union invades eastern Poland. The Battle of the Atlantic begins.

April: Germany invades Denmark and Norway; Allied troops land in Norway.

May: Germany invades Luxembourg, the Netherlands, Belgium, and France; Allied troops are evacuated at Dunkirk.

June: Allied troops leave Norway; Italy enters the war; France signs an armistice with Germany; Italy bombs Malta in the Mediterranean.

July: German submarines (U-boats) inflict heavy losses on Allied convoys in the Atlantic; The Battle of Britain begins.

September: Luftwaffe air raids begin the Blitz—the bombing of British cities; Italian troops advance from Libya into Egypt.

October: Italy invades Greece.

December: British troops defeat the Italians at Sidi Barrani, Egypt.

1941   **January:** Allied units capture Tobruk in Libya.

February: Rommel's Afrika Korps arrive in Tripoli.

March: The Afrika Korps drive British troops back from El Agheila.

April: Axis units invade Yugoslavia; German forces invade Greece; the Afrika Korps besiege Tobruk.

June: German troops invade the Soviet Union.

September: Germans besiege Leningrad and attack Moscow.

December: Japanese aircraft attack the U.S. Pacific Fleet at Pearl Harbor; Japanese forces invade the Philippines, Malaya, and Thailand, and defeat the British garrison in Hong Kong.

1942   **January:** Japan invades Burma; Rommel launches a new offensive in Libya; Allied troops leave Malaya.

February: Singapore surrenders to the Japanese.

April: The Bataan Peninsula in the Philippines falls to the Japanese.

May: U.S. and Japanese fleets clash at the Battle of the Coral Sea.

June: The U.S. Navy defeats the Japanese at the Battle of Midway; Rommel recaptures Tobruk.

September–October: Allied forces defeat Axis troops at El Alamein, Egypt, the first major Allied victory of the war.

November: U.S. and British troops land in Morocco and Algeria.

1943

February: The German Sixth Army surrenders at Stalingrad; the Japanese leave Guadalcanal in the Solomon Islands.

May: Axis forces in Tunisia surrender.

July: The Red Army wins the Battle of Kursk; Allied troops land on the Italian island of Sicily.

August: German forces occupy Italy; the Soviets retake Kharkov.

September: Allied units begin landings on mainland Italy; Italy surrenders, prompting a German invasion of northern Italy.

November: U.S. carrier aircraft attack Rabaul in the Solomon Islands.

1944

January: The German siege of Leningrad ends.

February: U.S. forces conquer the Marshall Islands.

March: The Soviet offensive reaches the Dniester River; Allied aircraft bomb the monastery at Monte Cassino in Italy.

June: U.S. troops enter the city of Rome; D-Day–the Allied invasion of northern Europe; U.S. aircraft defeat the Japanese fleet at the Battle of the Philippine Sea.

July: Soviet tanks enter Poland.

August: Japanese troops retreat in Burma; Allied units liberate towns in France, Belgium, and the Netherlands.

October: The Japanese suffer defeat at the Battle of Leyte Gulf.

December: German troops counterattack in the Ardennes.

1945

January: The U.S. Army lands on Luzon in the Philippines; most of Poland and Czechoslovakia are liberated by the Allies.

February: U.S. troops land on Iwo Jima; Soviet troops strike west across Germany; the U.S. Army heads toward the Rhine River.

April: U.S. troops land on the island of Okinawa; Mussolini is shot by partisans; Soviet troops assault Berlin; Hitler commits suicide.

May: All active German forces surrender.

June: Japanese resistance ends in Burma and on Okinawa.

August: Atomic bombs are dropped on Hiroshima and Nagasaki; Japan surrenders.

GLOSSARY

Allies One of the two groups of combatants in the war. The main Allies were Britain, the Soviet Union, the United States, British Empire troops, and free forces from occupied nations.

Axis One of the two groups of combatants in the war. The leading Axis powers were Germany, Italy, and Japan.

Blitz The German bombing campaign against British cities from September 1940 to May 1941.

censored Having been changed for reasons such as national security.

colonies Countries governed by another country.

communism A political system in which economic activity is controlled by the state and individual freedom is limited.

conscription Forcing someone to enter the service of the state.

decolonization The process of allowing colonies to become self-governing.

demobilization Sending military personnel home after a war.

empire A group of a number of countries governed by a single country.

fascism An authoritarian and militaristic form of government.

goosestep A method of marching in which the legs do not bend at the knee.

hardware Weapons, vehicles, and other pieces of military equipment.

independence The state of self-government for a people or nation.

isolationism A policy of avoiding involvement in overseas affairs.

morale The positive belief and enthusiasm of an individual or group of people.

morse code A code in which letters of the alphabet are represented by combinations of long or short signals of sound or light.

nationalist A person who believes his or her country should be independent.

neutral Not taking sides in a dispute or conflict.

patriotic Motivated by a deep love of one's country.

propaganda Information that is biased in order to promote a particular point of view.

prosthetics Artificial body parts.

puppet government A government that governs on behalf of the government of another country.

swastika A cross with arms broken at right angles, used as a symbol by the Nazi Party.

FURTHER RESOURCES

Books

Cromwell, Sharon. *GI Joe in World War II* (We' the People). Compass Point Books, 2008.

George, Enzo. *World War II in Europe and North Africa: Preserving Democracy* (Voices of War). Cavendish Square Publishing, 2014.

George, Enzo. *World War II in the Pacific: War with Japan* (Voices of War). Cavendish Square Publishing, 2014.

Global Chaos (World War II). Marshall Cavendish Corporation, 2010.

Hynson, Colin. *World War II: A Primary Source History* (In Their Own Words). Gareth Stevens Publishing, 2005.

Samuels, Charlie. *Soldiers* (World War II Sourcebooks). Brown Bear Books, 2012.

Websites

www.ducksters.com/history/world_war_ii/
Ducksters.com links to articles about the war.

www.historyonthenet.com/ww2/home_front.htm
History.com page of links about aspects of World War II.

www.socialstudiesforkids.com/subjects/worldwarii.htm/
Index of articles about U.S. involvement in the conflict.

http://www.pbs.org/thewar/
PBS pages on the war to support the Ken Burns' film, *The War.*

http://www.pbs.org/wgbh/amex/dday/timeline/
Timeline of the war on PBS pages from The American Experience.

Publisher's Note
Our editors have carefully reviewed the websites that appear on this page to ensure that they are suitable for students. Many websites change frequently, however, and we cannot guarantee that a site's future contents will continue to meet our high standards of quality. Be advised that students should be closely supervised whenever they access the Internet.

INDEX